At Home with Science

Splish! Splosh!

Why do we wash?

Written by Janice Lobb
Illustrated by Peter Utton

KING*f*ISHER

NEW YORK

KINGFISHER
Larousse Kingfisher Chambers Inc.
95 Madison Avenue
New York, New York 10016

First published in 2000
10 9 8 7 6 5 4 3 2 1

ITR(1DS)/1299/FR(FR)/128MAWA

Created by Snapdragon Publishing Ltd.
Copyright © Snapdragon Publishing Ltd. 2000

LIBRARY OF CONGRESS CATALOGING-IN-PUBLICATION DATA
Lobb, Janice.
    Splish! Splosh! Why do we wash?/by Janice Lobb; illustrated
by Peter Utton.—1st ed.
        p. cm. — (At home with science)
    Summary: Explains the importance of bathing and showering
and examines the scientific principles that can be demonstrated
during such activities. Includes experiments.
    ISBN 0-7534-5244-8
    1. Baths—Health aspects—Juvenile literature. 2. Children—
Health and hygiene—Juvenile literature. [1. Baths. 2. Cleanliness.
3. Water—Experiments. 4. Experiments.] I. Utton, Peter, ill. II.
Title. III. At home with science (New York, N.Y.)

RA780.L63 2000
500—dc21
                                    99-049920

Printed in Hong Kong

Author Janice Lobb
Illustrators Peter Utton and Ann Savage (page 24)

For Snapdragon
Editorial Director Jackie Fortey
Art Director Chris Legee
Designer Richard Rowan

For Kingfisher
Series Editor Camilla Reid
Series Art Editor Mike Buckley

Contents

About this book

Lying back in a hot, bubbly bath doesn't feel like science, does it? Well it is! So is brushing your teeth, drying yourself... and even flushing the toilet! This book is about the science that happens around you every day in the bathroom. Keep your eyes open and you'll be surprised by what you discover!

Which?

How?

Where?

What if?

Why?

Hall of Fame

Archie and his friends are here to help you. They are each named after famous scientists—apart from Bob the (rubber) Duck, who is just a young scientist like you!

Archie
ARCHIMEDES (287–212 B.C.)
The Greek scientist Archimedes figured out why things float or sink while he was in the bathtub. According to the story, he was so pleased that he leaped up, shouting "Eureka!" which means "I've done it!"

Frank
BENJAMIN FRANKLIN (1706–1790)
Besides being one of the most important figures in American history, he was also a noted scientist. In a dangerous experiment in which he flew a kite in a storm, he proved that lightning is actually electricity.

Marie
MARIE CURIE (1867–1934)
Girls did not go to college in Poland where Marie Curie grew up, so she went to Paris to study. Later, she worked on radioactivity and received two Nobel prizes for her discoveries, in 1903 and 1911.

Dot
DOROTHY HODGKIN (1910–1994)
Dorothy Hodgkin was a British scientist, who made many important discoveries about molecules and atoms, the tiny particles that make up everything around us. She was given the Nobel prize for Chemistry in 1964.

See for yourself!

1 Read about the science in your bathroom, then try the "See for yourself!" experiments to discover how it works. In science, experiments are used to find or show the answers.

2 Carefully read the instructions for each experiment, making sure you follow the numbered steps in the correct order.

3 Here are some of the things you will need. Have everything ready before you start each experiment.

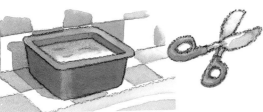

Shallow bucket   Scissors   Plastic bottle

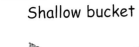

Tape   Spoon   Fabric scraps   Glass bowl

4 Safety first!

Some scientists take risks to make their discoveries, but our experiments are safe. Just make sure that you tell an adult what you are doing and ask them to help you if you see the red warning sign.

Amazing facts

WOW!

You'll notice that some words are written in *italics*. You can learn more about them in the glossary at the end of the book. And if you want to find out some amazing facts, keep an eye out for the "Wow!" features.

Keep an eye out for useful tips!

Have fun!

5

What is a wave?

A wave is simply *energy* moving from one place to another. Sometimes we can see waves, like the ones that move through water. Other waves, such as sound waves, that travel through air, are invisible. A wave does not happen by itself—something has to start it off. We call this a *disturbance*.

What makes big waves?

Big hands!

As energy passes through water, the water moves up and down.

The highest part of the wave is called the crest

The water doesn't move forward with the wave, so Bob just bobs up and down in the same place.

The lowest part of the wave is called the trough

See for yourself!

1 Make your own bathtime waves by tapping the surface of the water. Try a gentle tap, followed by a hard one. What do you see?

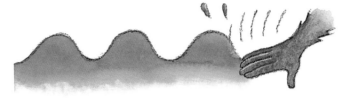

2 Tap the water quickly several times. You should find that this makes waves with crests that are close together. Now try tapping slowly.

Quick taps

Slow taps

3 What happens when a wave reaches the side of the bathtub? It doesn't disappear—it bounces off and comes back. This is called *reflection*.

WOW!

Giant ocean waves

Ocean waves are caused by the wind. A gentle wind makes small waves, while strong winds make big, high waves. Sometimes, when an earthquake happens under the sea, a huge wave called a tsunami is created. A tsunami can be over 100 feet high when it reaches the shore. This kind of wave can be very dangerous.

Be careful not to make your own tsunami!

How does soap get me clean?

Your skin produces oil to keep it smooth and flexible. But when you get dirt on your skin, the dirt sticks to this oil and water alone will not wash it off. This is because oil and water do not mix, so water just rolls off oily, dirty skin. Soap gets your skin clean because it acts as a *detergent*.

What did the soap say to the bubbles?

Don't forget to foam!

Soap in action

A detergent works by allowing the oil and water to mix.

The soap breaks the dirty oil up into little drops and holds it in the water. This mixture is called an *emulsion*.

You can then wash the dirt and oil off your skin, leaving you nice and clean!

See for yourself!

1 Half fill a clear plastic bottle (a small soda bottle, for example) with water, then add a thin layer of cooking oil. Hold the bottle up to the light and look through the side. Do the oil and water mix?

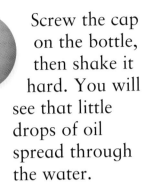

2 Screw the cap on the bottle, then shake it hard. You will see that little drops of oil spread through the water.

3 Stop shaking and leave the mixture for a couple of minutes. Watch what happens to the oil and water. How have the drops of oil changed?

4 Now add a squirt of shampoo to the bottle, put the cap on, and shake it up again. The water stays cloudy because the shampoo has mixed the oil and water into an emulsion.

Sticky scum

If you use soap in hard water (see page 12), you get a different kind of emulsion. It is thicker and stickier and you need a lot more soap to make a lather. When it reaches the edge of the tub, instead of just washing away, it leaves a ring of *soap scum* on the side of the bathtub. Yuck!

WOW!

Be careful not to slip!

Why does a boat float?

Have you noticed that some things float and other things sink? Whether an object floats or sinks depends on how heavy it is and what size it is. Together, weight and size make up an object's *density*. Anything that is denser than water sinks to the bottom of the tub. Air is less dense than water, so it always floats. A toy boat floats because it is hollow and the air inside it makes it float. Bob floats for the same reason—but Archie sinks!

What sinks?

Test some of these objects to see if they float or sink.

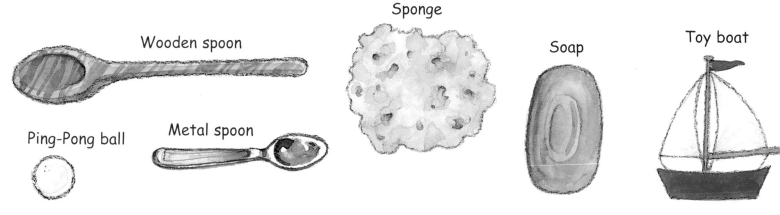

Ping-Pong ball

Wooden spoon

Metal spoon

Sponge

Soap

Toy boat

See for yourself!

Hollow objects float because the air inside them makes their overall density less than the density of water. A plastic cup is denser than water, but with air inside it, it floats.

1 Take a clear plastic cup and put it upside down in the water. As you push it down, notice that no water enters the cup.

2 Keep pushing down until the cup is under the water. Does it get harder to push down? Now try tilting the cup up a little. Do you see air bubbles escaping?

Air bubbles

3 With the air gone from inside the cup, it is now denser than water, so it sinks.

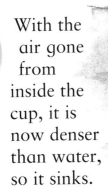

WOW!

Weight of boat | Upthrust of water | Weight of boat

Water forces

When a boat is put in water, the water pushes against it with a force called *upthrust*. If the weight of the boat is less than the force of the upthrust, then the boat stays afloat. If the weight of the boat is greater than the upthrust, then the boat will sink.

If your boat fills up with water it will sink, Bob!

What is hard water?

All water may look the same, but did you know that some water is *hard* and other water is *soft*? Hard water is found in places where there are chalk or limestone rocks under ground. Rainwater picks up tiny pieces of a mineral called *calcium* from these rocks. This is carried by the water and we say it has become "hard." Pure rainwater has no calcium in it, so we call it "soft" water.

What did the water say to the soap?

Don't get into a lather!

Blowing bubbles

Get your hands soapy, make a big "O" with your thumb and finger, then try to blow a bubble!

If the water is hard, it will be difficult to make soap bubbles. Hard water also leaves a ring of soap scum around the edge of the bathtub.

See for yourself!

1 Half fill a jar with soft water, such as rainwater. Add a small piece of soap and shake the jar. How much lather does it make?

Lather
Rainwater
Soap

2 Now make your own hard water by putting a piece of chalk in another jar, this time filled with soda water. Wait for the chalk to dissolve.

Soda water
Chalk

3 Put a piece of soap into this chalky, hard water and shake it up. Do you see lather or scum? You should see scum.

Scum

Soap

4 Finally, shake up some soap in a jar of your home tap water. Is it hard or soft?

If you see lather, the water is soft. If you see scum, the water is hard.

Shower block

When hard water is heated, the calcium in it comes out of the water. You can see this as a layer of *limescale* on the inside of a teakettle. Limescale can also block up the holes in your shower and keep it from working.

WOW!

Calcium in hard water helps give you strong teeth and bones!

13

Why do I turn red in the tub?

Why does my skin look red?

Because it's trying to be cool!

When you take a hot bath, the *nerves* in your skin tell your body that it is getting warm. To keep you from overheating, your body starts to cool itself by bringing the blood to the surface of the skin, where it can give off heat. If your skin looks red or flushed, it is because you can see this blood just under the surface. In hot weather, or when you have a fever, you turn red for the same reason.

Tiny tubes

Blood flows through tiny tubes called *capillaries*. If there is a lot of blood in them, your skin gets hot. If there isn't, your skin cools down.

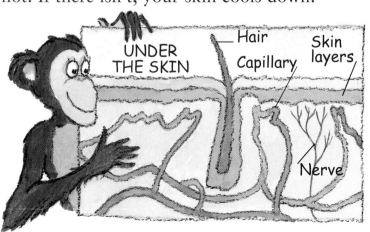

UNDER THE SKIN — Hair — Capillary — Skin layers — Nerve

Heat Heat Heat

Animals in hot countries need to keep cool. Although elephants do not turn red, they do have big ears with a large area of skin that help them lose heat.

See for yourself! ✋

1 Line up three bowls. Put ice-cold water into one, warm water into the second, and very warm water into the third.

Ice-cold water

Warm water

Very warm water

2 Ask an adult to check that the very warm water is not too hot to touch. It should feel like very warm bathwater.

Very warm water

3 Put one hand in the cold water and your other hand in the very warm water. Now move both hands into the warm water.

Cold water

Very warm water

4 Your two hands feel very different because, at first, the nerves can only tell you that there have been changes in temperature. Eventually, they adjust to the new temperature.

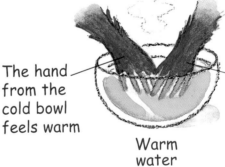
The hand from the cold bowl feels warm

The hand from the very warm bowl feels cold

Warm water

Red for go!

WOW!

Blood gets its color from a substance called *hemoglobin*. Hemoglobin carries oxygen around the body to give us energy. It contains the mineral iron, which is what makes the hemoglobin red. Amazingly, your body contains enough iron to make a nail!

Check the temperature of the bath or shower before getting in.

How does a shower work?

Flowing water is pushed along by the force of the water behind it. This force is called *water pressure*. When water comes out of a faucet it stays together as a single stream, but in a shower, the water has to come out of a lot of tiny holes. Forcing the same amount of water out of small holes increases the water pressure and gives you a lot of little jets of water. And because the holes in a showerhead are all at slightly different angles, the water spreads out in different directions.

What has a head but no neck?

A shower!

Feel the pressure

Water pressure

If you put your hand close to the showerhead, you can feel the water pressure.

Frank's shower has an electric pump to help push the water up and out. Bob has a tank above his shower. The water is pushed out by the pressure of the water in the tank.

16

See for yourself! ✋

1 Find an empty plastic soda bottle and ask an adult to make four holes in a line from top to bottom (see page 32 for instructions). This is tricky, so don't try to do it by yourself.

2 When you are taking a bath, fill the bottle with bathwater and stand it up on the side of the bathtub.

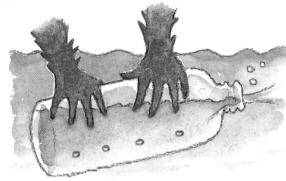

3 The water pressure is greatest at the bottom of the bottle, so the lowest jet travels farthest.

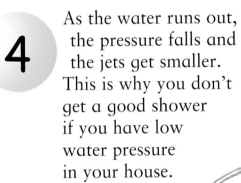

4 As the water runs out, the pressure falls and the jets get smaller. This is why you don't get a good shower if you have low water pressure in your house.

WOW!

Superjets

When water is forced out through a small hole it travels farther than if it is pushed through a larger one. You can try this with a hose by putting your finger over the hole at the end. How far you can make the water travel?

Save water! A shower uses half as much water as a bath.

17

Why does the water get cold?

If you have ever taken a very long bath, you will know that the water soon cools down and you start to feel a little bit chilly. This is because of a process called *evaporation*. Over time, some of the surface water escapes into the air as tiny *particles* called *water vapor*. As this water evaporates, it takes the heat from the water with it into the colder bathroom air, making the bathwater cool down and the bathroom warm up.

What kind of water never freezes?

Boiling water!

Why do mirrors mist up?

Invisible water vapor hits a cold mirror...

and turns back into drops of liquid water.

Feel the wetness on the mirror. This is called *condensation*.

Water vapor

Water drops

See for yourself!

1 Dry one of your hands and wet the other one in the bathtub.

2 Hold your index fingers in front of your mouth and blow on them.

3 As the water evaporates from your wet finger, it takes the heat from your finger with it, making it feel colder. The longer you blow, the colder it feels. Your dry finger does not feel as cold.

4 Hold your fingers against your face. Do they feel different?

Your dry finger will feel quite warm

Your wet finger should feel much colder

Full steam ahead!

Steam is hot water vapor that comes from water when it boils (at 212°F). We see steam when it condenses in the air. Steam can be useful—a steam iron is very good at getting the wrinkles out of clothes.

WOW!

When we dry our hair the water evaporates!

Why do I have to brush my teeth?

Although teeth are hard, they are actually living things, and grow from the jawbone out through the gums. *Baby teeth* start growing when we are babies. Then, as we get older, they fall out and are replaced by adult teeth. After that, we do not grow any more teeth, so it is important to take care of them. Brushing helps keep them clean and healthy.

What did the teeth say to the sandwich?

Nice to eat you!

Different kinds of teeth

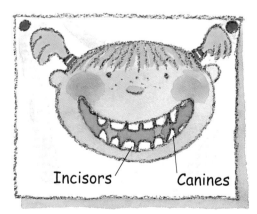

Incisors   Canines

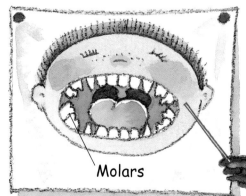

Molars

The shiny white surface of the tooth is hard *enamel*. It protects the tooth and gives it sharp cutting edges

Front teeth, called incisors, are for cutting and nibbling food. Canines are pointed teeth for tearing food.

The teeth at the back of your mouth are called molars. They are for grinding up large pieces of food.

See for yourself!

1 How many teeth do you have? If you have not lost any yet, you probably have 20 baby teeth. Adults have 32 teeth.

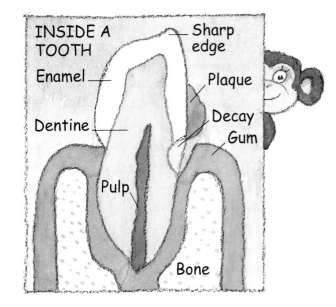

INSIDE A TOOTH

Enamel

Dentine

Pulp

Sharp edge

Plaque

Decay

Gum

Bone

2 When one of your baby teeth falls out, take a careful look at it. It is hollow underneath, where the blood vessels kept it alive, and has shiny, white enamel on top.

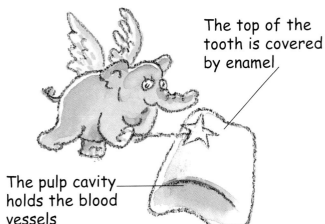

The top of the tooth is covered by enamel

The pulp cavity holds the blood vessels

Plaque attack!

WOW!

A tooth has three layers—soft pulp in the center, a hard layer of dentine in the middle, and a tough coating of enamel on the outside. If you don't brush, a layer of *plaque* forms on your teeth. Eventually this hardens and starts to make acids that attack your teeth and gums. This can lead to cavities that will need to be filled.

Remember to brush your teeth twice a day.

3 Put your tooth in a glass of soda and leave it for several days. As the sugary acid attacks the tooth you will see that it starts to turn brown and decay.

How does a towel get me dry?

The material that towels are made of is *porous*, which means that it *absorbs*, or soaks up, water easily. If you look closely at a dry towel you will see that it is made of a woven cotton material that is covered with little loops. These loops are like tiny pockets full of air. When you wrap yourself in the towel, the water is drawn into the loops and the air is pushed out. So the towel gets wet— and you get dry!

What gets wetter as it dries?

A towel!

Why doesn't Bob get wet?

Bob doesn't get wet because he's *waterproof*, which means that he cannot absorb water. Instead, the water forms drops on his surface, then runs off. If you drop water onto your hand you'll see that you are waterproof too. That why you don't get soggy when you take a bath!

See for yourself!

1 Collect things made of different materials, such as an old towel or washcloth, cotton or wool fabric, newspaper, a wad of cotton, and a plastic bag.

2 Cut them into strips about 4 inches long and tape them to a plastic ruler. Hold the ruler over a bowl of water, with all the pieces just touching the water.

3 Watch each strip to see what happens to the water. Which one soaks up the most water?

Squeezy skeletons

Sponges are porous because they are full of holes that can soak up a lot of water. A natural sponge is the soft skeleton of a creature that once lived under the sea. Sponges are collected in warm seas by divers, or pulled into boats with hooks. Most people today use artificial sponges.

Towels take time to dry. Remember to hang them up!

How does the toilet flush?

Some toilets work using the *siphon* effect. When you push the handle down to flush the toilet, it starts water flowing from the tank into the bowl. Although the water always wants to flow from the tank into the bowl, it can't because a bent pipe blocks its way. By activating the siphon effect, water can flow up the pipe, and then down into the bowl.

Why did the toilet flush?

Because it saw the tub's bottom!

Inside a toilet

As the handle goes down, a lever inside pulls up the disk. One side of the pipe fills with water and pushes the air out of the way.

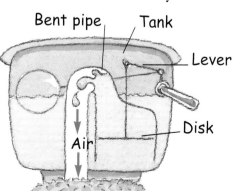

Bent pipe Tank

Lever

Disk

Air

When the water gets up to the bend at the top of the siphon, it starts to flow down the other side of the pipe.

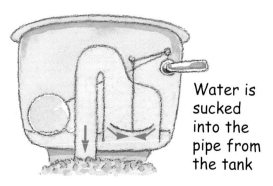

Water is sucked into the pipe from the tank

Once the water has started flowing, it can't stop until the tank is empty. Then the tank fills up again, ready to flush.

Air

See for yourself!

1 To see how a siphon works, first fill a shallow bucket with water, then place it on the edge of a bathtub full of water.

2 Put one end of a piece of plastic tubing in the bucket and the other end in the bathtub. The tube is full of air so water cannot flow through it.

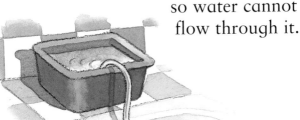

3 Now put one end of the tube under the bathwater and fill it up. Cover one end of the tube with your thumb and put it back in the bucket. Keep the other end in the bathtub.

Make sure there are no air bubbles in the tube

4 Now take your thumb away and watch the water go! Because there is no air between the two water levels, the water is siphoned out and the bucket empties.

The first flush!

WOW!

The flushing toilet was invented by Sir John Harington in about 1591. He built one for Queen Elizabeth I at one of her palaces in England. In those days a toilet was called a jakes or a privy. Today we just say that we are going to the bathroom or the restroom.

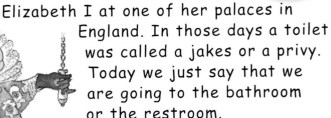

Remember to wash your hands after going to the bathroom!

What is the bathtub made of?

Most bathtubs look alike, but some are made of iron, some are made of *steel*, and others are made of *plastic*. A bathtub made of iron doesn't look as if it is made of metal because it is coated with a layer of glassy enamel. Other things in the bathroom that are made of iron may be covered in paint or *chrome*, to keep them from rusting.

What did one magnet say to the other magnet?

You're very attractive!

The magnet test

Use a magnet to find out what material your tub is made of. If it is iron or steel, the magnet will stick. The enamel on the surface will not stop it from working.

If the tub is made of plastic, the magnet will fall off. See what else in the bathroom attracts the magnet. Are the water pipes or the radiator made of iron?

See for yourself!

1 Find out what materials things are made of just by touching them. Hold a plastic object, such as a tumbler. It should feel warm.

A tumbler feels warm because plastic is a poor heat conductor

2 When you touch metal objects, they feel cold. Unlike plastic, metal takes heat away from your hand quickly. It is a good heat *conductor*.

An iron bathtub feels cold

3 Touch other materials in the bathroom. What are they made of? Do they feel warm or cold?

4 Which materials are natural (like wood) and which are synthetic (like steel, glass, and plastic)?

Hip! Hip! Hurray!

WOW!

Before houses had bathrooms, people took hip baths in their bedrooms. A hip bath was usually made of iron and had no faucets or drains. The water had to be carried to the bath in buckets. It was quite cozy to take a bath in your bedroom in front of a roaring fire.

Remember to clean the tub after your bath.

What can I see in the mirror?

When is the right side the wrong side?

What you see when you look in a mirror is not yourself, but a reflection or *mirror image* of yourself. Strange as it may seem, you don't see yourself as other people see you. They see you the "right" way. If you look at your reflection and a picture of yourself at the same time, you will see the difference.

When you look in a mirror!

Bouncing light!

Without light, we cannot see anything. We see an object because light travels from a source (the sun or, as shown here, a flashlight), bounces off the object, and then comes to our eyes.

Light rays travel in straight lines

Light rays bounce off the mirror

When light bounces off a smooth, shiny surface, more of it bounces back to you than from other objects. This is why you see a reflection.

See for yourself!

1 Stand close to a mirror, so that you can touch it. Then move it as far away as you can. The image moves too.

2 Stay still for a minute and look at your image.

It will seem to be the same distance behind the mirror as you are in front of it.

3 Wave your left hand. Which hand is the image waving? Is it the right or the left?

WOW!

Magic mirrors

Carnival mirrors can do strange things to your reflection! Look at yourself in both sides of a spoon. Do you look smaller when the spoon curves in or out?

Use a mirror to read this message!

-Good-bye!

29

Bathroom quiz

1 What is the highest part of a wave called?
a) A crust
b) A crest
c) A trough

2 What do you get when you mix soap, oil, and water?
a) An emulsion
b) An illusion
c) A detergent

3 What substance does hard water contain that soft water does not?
a) Air
b) Soap
c) Calcium

4 What happens when water vapor hits a cold surface?
a) It condenses
b) It evaporates
c) Nothing

5 What do you call the teeth you use for nibbling?
a) Incisors
b) Molars
c) Canines

6 Water is pushed through the holes of a shower by what?
a) Water vapor
b) Water pressure
c) Upthrust

7 Materials that absorb water are described as being what?
a) Waterproof
b) Plastic
c) Porous

8 Which of these substances will a magnet stick to?
a) Iron
b) Plastic
c) Marble

9 What is the name of the tiny tubes that carry blood under the skin?
a) Nerves
b) Hairs
c) Capillaries

10 When light bounces off a mirror, what happens to it?
a) It is absorbed
b) It is reflected
c) It condenses

Answers on page 32

Glossary

Absorb
To soak up a liquid.

Baby teeth
Small, first teeth in mammals (like us!) that fall out and are replaced by larger adult teeth.

Calcium
A mineral found in rocks such as chalk and limestone.

Capillaries
The smallest type of blood vessels, which carry blood and form fine networks under the skin's surface.

Chrome (or chromium)
A shiny metal used to coat metals such as iron to keep them from rusting.

Condensation
Water formed when water vapor comes in contact with a cold surface.

Conductor
Any material that can transfer heat without moving.

Density
The amount of a substance contained in a particular space.

Detergent
A substance such as soap that allows dirt and oils to mix and be washed away with water.

Disturbance
The movement of something from its original position, which gives out energy as it does so.

Emulsion
A mixture of small drops of one type of liquid in another liquid.

Enamel
1) A hard, shiny substance that covers teeth. 2) A hard, shiny substance used to cover metallic surfaces.

Energy
The ability to do work, or to make something happen.

Evaporation
When a liquid such as water turns into vapor by being heated.

Hemoglobin
A substance found in blood that contains iron and carries oxygen around the body.

Hard water
Water that does not lather with soap because it contains a lot of calcium.

Limescale
A solid chalky material that comes out of hard water when it is heated.

Mirror image
The reversed picture you see when you look in a shiny surface.

Nerves
Fibers in the body that carry messages from your senses to the brain, and give instructions to your muscles.

Particle
A very small piece of something.

Plaque
A buildup of bacteria that sticks to the teeth and causes tooth decay.

Plastic
A material, made from the chemicals in oil, that can be molded into any shape.

Porous
Full of very small holes that are filled with air, so they can absorb liquids.

Reflection
The bouncing of light or water waves back off a surface.

Siphon
A bent tube that allows water to be move up past a high point to a lower level.

Soap scum
A thick emulsion of dirt, water, and oil, that forms when you wash with soap in hard water.

Soft water
Water, such as rainwater, with little or no calcium in it.

Steel
A strong, shiny metal that is a mix of iron and other metals.

Upthrust
The upward push of water that helps objects float.

Water pressure
A push moving through a body of water, when it is squeezed from outside.

Waterproof
Something that is waterproof does not let water pass through it.

Water vapor
Free water particles that move around in the air after water has evaporated.

Index

Answers to the Bathroom quiz on page 30
1 b **2** a **3** c **4** a **5** a **6** b **7** c **8** a **9** c **10** b

 For adults only: To make a hole in a plastic bottle, heat the end of a skewer over a flame before piercing the side of the bottle.